Headwork Anthologies 1

Chris

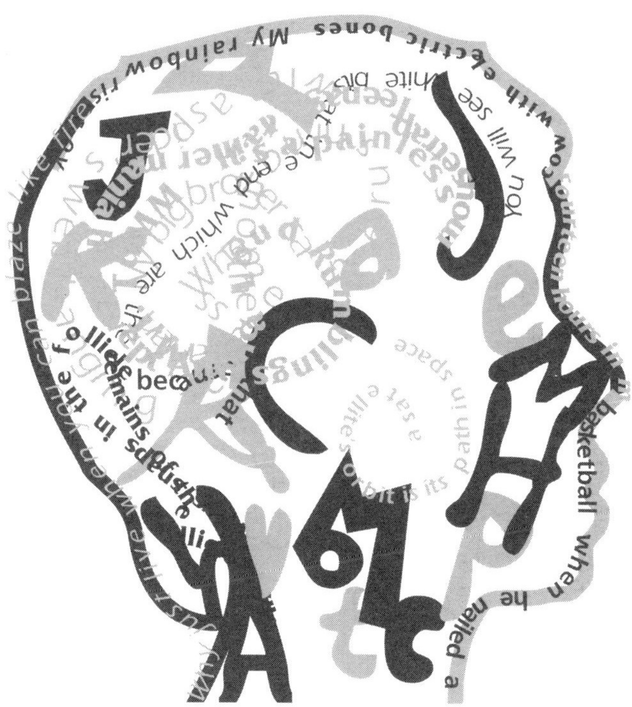

Oxford University Press

Oxford University Press, Great Clarendon Street,
Oxford OX2 6DP

Oxford New York
Athens Auckland Bangkok Bogota Bombay
Buenos Aires Calcutta Cape Town Dar es Salaam
Delhi Florence Hong Kong Istanbul Karachi
Kuala Lumpur Madras Madrid Melbourne
Mexico City Nairobi Paris Singapore
Taipei Tokyo Toronto

and associated companies
in Berlin Ibadan

Oxford is a trade mark of Oxford University Press

ISBN 019 833396 X
Printed and bound in Great Britain by
Scotprint Ltd, Musselburgh

Note for teachers

Headwork Anthologies, like the other books in the *Headwork* series, are designed to help students develop basic reading and writing skills.

The *Anthologies* require the students to respond to a wide range of material including stories, poems, articles, cartoons, and photographs. Students are asked to demonstrate comprehension of a text by turning it into a diagram or cartoon. A number of tasks test the students' literal comprehension, but the major emphasis is on evaluative responses: Why did X do Y? What did X feel when Y happened?

Many tasks require students to express an opinion, to compare these opinions with those in the text or to compare and evaluate a range of opinions. Students are also encouraged to look for connections between contrasting items on the same spread.

The table below shows main categories of tasks offered and their pages numbers.

Task	Pages
Creative writing Writing stories, poems, riddles, diaries, letters, etc.	5, 7, 9, 13, 17, 19, 21, 25, 29, 31, 35, 51, 57, 59, 61
Factual writing Articles, letters, diaries, adverts, brochures, etc.	7, 11, 25, 27, 33 39, 43, 45, 47, 49, 51, 53, 59, 63
Writing dialogue Scripting conversations. Using these in role play.	7, 9, 11, 37
Offering/defending an opinion Contrasting and appreciating differing points of view.	5, 11, 13, 27, 31, 35, 41, 47, 55
Responding to pictures Evaluating cartoons, diagrams, photographs. Responding via drawings, collage, cartoons, etc.	5, 17, 21, 23, 29, 41, 43, 49, 57, 41
Research skills Survey and interviews. Reference work, research, and recording. Gathering data from pupils and adults.	13, 15, 23, 25, 31, 33, 37, 51, 53, 55, 59
Looking at language Word play, puns, ambiguities. Patterns in language.	11, 13, 15, 17, 19, 21, 23, 25, 41, 43, 47

Contents

1 *Tooth and Claw* 4

2 *What's in a Name?* 12

3 *Mix Ups* 18

4 *Me, Myself, I* 28

5 *A Sporting Chance* 38

6 *Home Sweet Home?* 48

7 *Machine World* 58

Tooth and Claw

Leopard

Gentle hunter
his tail plays on the ground
while he crushes the skull.

Beautiful death
who puts on a spotted robe
when he goes to his victim.

Playful killer
whose loving embrace
splits the antelope's heart.

Yoruba Poem

Four Little Tigers

Four little tigers
Sitting in a tree;
One became a lady's coat –
Now there's only three.

Three little tigers
'Neath a sky of blue:
One became a rich man's rug –
Now there's only two.

Two little tigers
Sleeping in the sun:
One a hunter's trophy made –
Now there's only one.

One little tiger
Waiting to be had:
Oops! He got the hunter first –
Aren't you kind of glad?

Frank Jacobs

Cleaning Ladies

Belly stuffed with dust and fluff,
The Hoover moos and drones,
Grazing down on the carpet pasture:
Cow with electric bones.

Up in the tree of a chair the cat
Switches off its purr,
Stretches, blinks: a neat pink tongue
Vacuum–cleans its fur.

Hot Dog,
Kit Wright

The Greater Cats

The greater cats with golden eyes
Stare out between the bars.
Deserts are there, and different skies,
And night with different stars.

Vita Sackville-West

Four little tigers

1 What did the hunters do with the three tigers they killed?

2 How did the fourth tiger trick the final hunter?

3 Tigers are an 'endangered species'. What does this mean? Why has this happened?

Cleaning ladies and Greater cats

1 Draw a cartoon to show the difference between the life-style of a 'caged' cat and a domestic cat. You might want to use thought bubbles and/or captions with your drawing.

2 Write two diaries: one for a big cat in a zoo, the other for a pet cat. Use these to compare a week in the life of a caged cat with that of a domestic cat. You could set it out like this:

Day of Week	Zoo cat	Domestic cat
Sunday	Very noisy Thousands of visitors	Slept until 10 a.m.
Monday		

3 Use the table to write a poem or story about a pet cat who climbs into a zoo one night and watches some 'big cats' pacing backwards and forwards in their cages.

Cat

My cat's tail
can dance or beckon
whilst he sleeps,
can wave or threaten,
fall or rise.

Warily
it lies awake,
all on its own;
he wakes,
it lies forgotten.
It lives a life alone,
quite separate –
or so it seems.

Could it be the place
where, secretly,
his life goes on?
A space to hide for ever
a million catty dreams?

Midnight Forest,
Judith Evans

Tigger and Lucky

Tigger the Terror was a cat who thought he was a dog. He lay in wait for people delivering things to his home in a Devon village, and he attacked three postmen, the milkman, the paperman, and even a cameraman who came to take his picture. Then the Post Office asked his owner to try to keep Tigger indoors when the letters arrived. A warning notice told visitors what to expect – a cat with a temper like a tiger.

★ ★ ★

Two men who were robbing a village sub-post office were frightened away by a black cat called Lucky. Lucky was in the garden when the men walked into the shop at Abbots Morton, in Worcestershire. The Post Mistress refused to hand over the money. Then, in came Lucky, who leapt on to the back of one of the robbers, sinking her claws into him. He yelled, and both men ran off, empty-handed.

And Finally,
John Craven and Eric Rowan

Some Cats were Kept on Leads

In Japan, cats were so precious that they were kept on leads until 1602, when by order of the Emperor they were released so that they could kill the vermin that were threatening the silk crop. In 1750, the first cat imported into Paraguay was sold for the enormous sum of one pound of solid gold.

1500 Fascinating Facts,
ed. Simon Goodenough

Cat

1 Do cats dream?

2 Why does the poet think the cat's tail is the place where a cat might hide 'a million catty dreams'?

3 Write a story or a poem about a cat that has nightmares. These nightmares could be about how cats were kept in Japan.

Cats on leads

You live in Paraguay in 1750. You are the auctioneer at the sale of the first cat ever to be imported into your country. What do you say about the cat to the crowd before you start the bidding?
Remember, most people in Paraguay have never seen a cat before. They will know nothing about its habits or diet. Will you tell the truth about the cat? Or do you make the cat out to be something mysterious, even magical?
Write down what you would say to get people to bid for the cat, using about 100 words.

Tigger and Lucky

1 Why are some cats (like Tigger) quite aggressive? Is it something in their nature, or is it because they have not been properly trained?

2 Imagine that the two cats live next door to each other. Write a conversation between Tigger and Lucky. It might start something like this:

Tigger: You'll never guess what happened to me yesterday...
Lucky: What?

3 The owners of Tigger and Lucky want to sell them. Write a 'Cat for Sale' postcard – the kind you see in your local newsagent – for either Tigger or Lucky. The card should say something about the character of the cat and the kind of owner it needs.

The Ten Most Popular Cats' Names in Great Britain

1 Sooty
2 Tiger
3 Smoky
4 Tigger
5 Whiskey
6 Kitty
7 Lucky
8 Suzie
9 Fluffy
10 Snowy

Based on a 1987 Kattomeat/Gallup Survey in which 4,000 people were questioned about their pets.
In equal 11th place are: Suky, Thomas and Tabby.

Top Ten of Everything,
Russell Ash

Thank you, Dad, for Everything

Thank you for laying the carpet, dad,
Thank you for showing us how,
But what is that lump in the middle, dad?
And why is it saying mia–ow?

The Fed-up Family Album,
Doug Macleod

Reasons for Having a Pet

A dog will guard the house against burglars.

A cat will keep mice away.

A pet will teach me to be kind to animals.

They're killing stray cats/dogs at the animal home.

A canary will tell us if there's a gas leak.

All my friends have got pets.

I want an Alsatian so that I can win Cruft's Dog Show, become rich and famous and then help you financially.

If you have an animal you get on *Blue Peter*.

A tortoise is no trouble and doesn't have to be taken for long walks.

I promise I'll look after it.

If we have a dog, next door's cat will stop coming into our garden.

And if you still don't like the fish/rabbit, we can always eat it.

If I had a parrot I could teach it to talk and hire it out for films.

Taking a dog for walks would be good exercise for me.

A dog would fetch your papers for you

A pet would be a friend for me.

A cockerel will wake me up in the morning and make sure I get up for school.

How to Handle Grown-ups,
Jim and Duncan Eldridge

A lot to learn – What sort of things does the adult cat have to teach the kitten?

Face to face – What's the cat thinking?

Chocolate Point? How did this cat get its name? Do you know the names of any other breeds of cat?

Cat's names

1 The top ten names are rather dull. Make a list of ten 'ear-catching' cat's names.

2 Pick any two names from your list and write a conversation between two cats who have been given these names by their owners.
Set the conversation out like this:

Cat A: What's your name?
Cat B: Wash and Brush up.
Cat A: That's a pretty stupid name.
Cat B: Yes, I've got a pretty stupid owner.

Thank you, Dad

Make up some more four line poems like this one. Keep the first and third lines the same. Change the second and last lines to fit other animals trapped under the carpet.
Start by making a list of as many animal noises as you can.

Reasons for having a pet

1 Which are the sensible reasons given for having a pet?

2 Which are the silly reasons?

3 Write a dialogue between a parent and child. The child wants a pet puppy and the parent does not. The child gives reasons why having a puppy would be a good idea. Each time the parent tries to put forward the opposite point of view.

Dogs to Get a Chip Off the Old Doc!

Canine trend-setters have gone hi-tech. So if you want your dog to carry maximum street cred – get him chipped! One swift painless injection is all it takes to ensure that if Rover goes a roaming you are sure to get him back.

Name and address discs are fine, but many owners either don't bother to get one, or if they do they tend to get lost. But now, the computer age has come to the rescue of dogs, owners, and all concerned with animal welfare.

Morecambe and District Animal Care is helping to pioneer 'dog-chipping' in Britain in conjunction with vets Hudson, Salmon, and Bottom.

A micro-chip, the size of a grain of rice is implanted in the scruff and the dog carries ID for life. The scheme, which costs £20 is tipped to become law.

All dogs handled by Animal Care, the RSPCA, city council dog wardens, and soon, it is hoped all local vets, will be chipped. Anyone wanting to join the scheme now can go to Animal Care's Scotforth kennels or ask their vet. Said vet Mr Richard Bottom: 'If we can give dogs identification we can solve a lot of the problems they cause, whether they get lost, stolen or whatever.

'A lost dog, picked up by the dog warden, brought to our surgery or the RSPCA will be scanned and its home traced.'

***Lancaster Citizen,* 11 October 1990**

Dog's Tale

A young American man called Scott Brant was out late one night when a large, playful puppy came loping along the road towards him. Scott stroked it and it snuggled up to him, so he took it home and gave it some food. He'd never seen a dog quite like it before but it seemed affectionate. There was only one problem – it kept ripping up his furniture, and it was growing very quickly. Eventually he telephoned his local vet to see what advice he could offer. The vet took one look at the 'puppy' and immediately called the zoo. Scott was very embarrassed to admit that he hadn't been able to tell the difference between a puppy and a four-month-old lion cub that had recently escaped from the zoo.

My Most Embarrassing Moment

BITE Foils Tiger

A women saved her 10-year-old daughter by biting a tiger in Kuwait Zoo, the Kuwaiti newspaper Al-Qabas reported yesterday. When the tiger reached from its cage and got the child's head between its paws, the mother bit it and pulled the girl free.

***Mrs Brown's Scrapbook,* Niki**

Dog's tale

1 Write a conversation that Scott Brant might have had with the vet. Set it out like this:

Vet: When did you first notice something was wrong?
Scott: When he roared at the postwoman!

2 Some people keep large 'cats' (tigers, lions, etc.) as household pets. Write 5 or 6 sentences giving your opinion on this. Do you think it is cruel, exciting, dangerous?

Bite foils tiger

1 Why did the tiger let go of the child?

2 Do you think the woman was brave?

3 Two reporters **A** and **B** have been sent to report on the 'Woman Bites Tiger' story. Reporter **A** works for a newspaper and **B** for TV news. Make a chart like this to show how the two reports would be different.

Newspaper report	Television report
Mainly words	*Mainly pictures*

4 Do you think the kind of language (words or phrases, length of sentences, etc.) used in the two reports would be the same? If not, in what ways might they be different?

Chip off the old doc

1 How will the dog-tagging scheme work?

2 What information should be stored on the micro-chip implanted in the dog?

3 What do you think are the main advantages and disadvantages of the scheme?

4 Design an advert for a company who do micro-chip implants on pets. Invent details, such as a name for your company, a logo, slogan, a list of prices for various animals, the benefits of the chip, etc.

What's in a Name?

Nomenclature

'What terrible names
Are 'Jamie' and 'James',
Thought Jim.
'Peter' is sweeter
And 'Patrick' is neater'.

But when he was christened,
Nobody listened
To him.

Peter Wesley-Smith

Well Named

A Montreal bank-clerk, appropriately named Gerry Cash, fell in love with one of his attractive colleagues and was delighted when she accepted his proposal of marriage. So Mr and Mrs Cash now work side by side in the bank. She was actually quite relieved. Her married name, Cash, is much more acceptable than her maiden name – Crook.

That's Life

Babies' Names

Jack *b* Originally a diminutive of JOHN, it is now used independently. It is also used generically for men, e.g. 'every man-jack', 'Jack Frost', 'Jack Tar', etc., *Dim.* JACKY.

Jacob *b* Hebrew; 'the supplanter'. *Dim.* JAKE.

Jacobina *g* Scottish feminine version of the above.

Jacqueline *g* French feminine version of JAQUES (JAMES). *Dim.* JACKIE.

James *b* Hebrew; derived from Ja'akob, 'a heel', because Jacob took his brother Esau by the heel in the womb. The French form, JAQUES, is occasionally found as a Christian name in England. The Irish version (SEAMUS) and the Scottish version (HAMISH) are also found. James has been a favourite royal name. *Dim.* JAMIE, JIM.

Jamesina *g* Scottish feminine version of the above.

Jan *b* Welsh form of JOHN, q.v.

Jane *g* Contraction of JOANNA, q.v. *Dim.* JANIE.

Janet, Jannet, Janette *g* Originally diminutives of JANE.

Janice *g* Hebrew; 'Gift of God'.

Japheth *b* Hebrew; 'may he expand'.

Jasmine *g* Flower name, originally Persian.

Jason *b* Greek; 'a healer'.

Jasper *b* Persian; 'master of the treasure'. The variant CASPAR, or KASPAR, is sometimes found.

Jean, Jeanne *g* Originally a Scottish variant of JANE and JOAN, it is now widely used independently and is one of the most popular girl's names. *Dim.* JEANIE, JEANETTE.

Naming Baby,
Eugene Stone

Nomenclature

Nomenclature means 'the way we name things'.

1 Imagine a law was passed that said: 'All children must be allowed to choose their own Christian name(s)'. In future, a child might be given a 'For-the-time-being' name when they are born. Then, when they are old enough, they could choose their own Christian name. Do you think such a law would be a good idea?

2 With 3 or 4 others in your group or class make a list of as many Christian names (female and male) as you can. Use this list to write a poem about changing names. It could be made up of rhyming couplets like this:

My best friend used to be called Cheryl.
Last week she changed her name to Meryl.

Babies' names

1 Make a list of all the different languages the names come from.

2 What do the abbreviations *b*, *g*, *Dim.* and *q.v.* mean?

3 What does 'derived from' mean?

4 Use a dictionary of names to investigate the origins of your own name and those of your friends and family.

Well named

1 Can you think of any other surnames that would have worked as well in this story?

e.g. The bank-clerk could have been called 'Shilling' or 'Pound'.

2 Make a table of names like this for other occupations:

Occupation	Appropriate name	Inappropriate name
Teacher	*Ms Bright*	*Ms Cane*

3 Pick a pair of names from the table and write a story like 'Well Named', about a couple who do the same job and get married.

4 Many women these days keep their own surname (maiden name) after they marry. Why do they do this?

5 Would you like to change one of your names? If so, what new name(s) would you pick and why?
(When you are 18 you may change your surname but not your forename or Christian name. Your name on your birth certificate *cannot* be changed.)

The Ten Commonest Surnames in Great Britain

1. Smith
2. Jones
3. Williams
4. Brown
5. Taylor
6. Davies/Davis
7. Evans
8. Thomas
9. Roberts
10. Johnson

Top Ten of Everything,
Russell Ash

Enough Smiths

There are enough Smiths in England and Wales to fill Wembley Stadium eight times over.

Would You Believe It?,
D. Sanders, Girling, Davies, and R. Sanders

Titles and Authors

The Working of an Electric Drill by Andy Gadget
Stand and Deliver: The Story of Dick Turpin by Ann Dover
Pet Owning by Ivor Dog
Bad Shooting by Miss A. Lot
Snake Breeding by Sir Pent
Doubt by R. U. Sure
Bed Time by I. M. Tired
What to Use When Cooking by U. Tensils
Who Saw Him Leave? by Wendy Go
Say Your Prayers by Neil Down
Something for the Toast by Margorie Nisgood
The Winner by Vic Tree
Help for a Jail Breaker by Freda Prisner
Sahara Journey by I. Rhoda Camel
The Painter by R. T. Stick
Loud Rumblings by M. T. Tumm
Old Furniture by Ann Teak
Ghosts by R. U. Scared
All About Dogs by K. Nine
Astronomy by I. C. Stars
Dinosaurs by Terry Dacktill
One Hundred Yards to the Bus Stop by Willy Makitt, illustrated by Betty Wont

The End,
ed. Richard Stanley

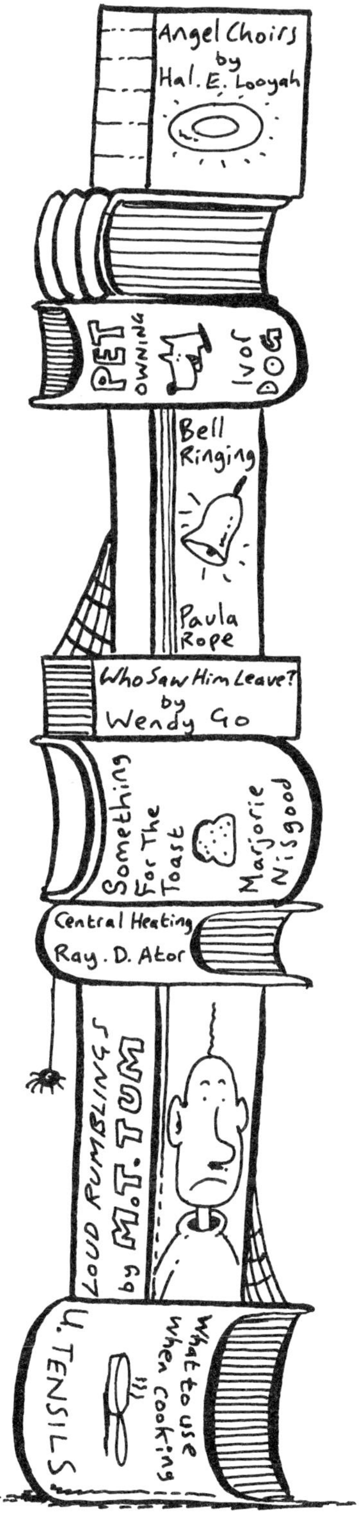

Ten commonest surnames

1 Why do you think are there so many people in Great Britain called Smith?

2 Do you know any common surnames from other countries, e.g. Shultz, Dupont, Hussein?

3 Many names (forenames and surnames) have meanings. Does your surname have a meaning? If you are unsure, look it up. There will be at least one book on names in your school or local library.

4 When parents name their children they have to be careful. Sometimes children can end up with unfortunate initials!

e.g. Fiona Amanda Thompson.

But sometimes a person's initials can be quite flattering.

e.g. Alice Claire Elsworth.

Invent some names for people with embarrassing and flattering initials. A book of names will help with this task.

5 Role play a situation in which two parents-to-be are arguing over what to call their baby. One parent wants to call it something *very* unusual. The other wants something more common. What decision do you come to?

Book titles and authors

1 Can you work out which each author's name is meant to sound like?

e.g. Andy Gadget is supposed to sound like 'handy gadget'.

2 Suggest some book titles for these authors: Mister Step, Bill Ding, Dinah Mite.

3 Pick one of the authors and titles from the list opposite and design a front cover for that book.

Private? No!

Private
No swimming
Allowed

Private?
No. Swimming
Allowed.

***Another Almanac of Words at Play,* W. R. Espry**

Rasher Than Need Be

A man was driving his friend along a country road when a car suddenly appeared round a corner, and on the wrong side of the road. Both drivers swerved and a collision was avoided. But the woman who was driving the car lowered the window and shouted, 'Pigs!'

Amazed by this unprovoked abuse, the man muttered, 'Women drivers,' turned the corner... and drove straight into a herd of pigs.

That's Life

More than One Meaning

The escaping convict dropped a bullet in his leg.
The escaping convict dropped, a bullet in his leg.

The butler stood by the door and called the guests' names as they arrived.
The butler stood by the door and called the guests names as they arrived.

Go slow, children.
Go slow – children.

I'm sorry you can't come with us.
I'm sorry. You can't come with us.

Do not break your bread, or roll in your soup.
Do not break your bread or roll in your soup.

Another Almanac of Words at Play,
W. R. Espry

***Rocking the Boat,* Helen Cusack**

More than one meaning

1 Sometimes the words we use have more than one meaning. Which word in the 'Rasher Than Need Be' story has a double meaning?

2 What is the double meaning in the 'Telly's Gone Funny' cartoon?

3 Explain the other double meanings on these pages.

4 Draw a cartoon or write a short story or poem about one or more of the phrases below with double meanings:

- Raining cats and dogs
- Dead lucky
- Drink like a fish
- Eat like a horse
- Drop off to sleep

Mix Ups

School Jokes

Teacher: Wayne, spell 'wrong'.
Wayne: R-O-N-G.
Teacher: That's wrong.
Wayne: Well that's what you asked for.

Teacher: John, give me a sentence with the word 'centimetre' in it.
John: Er, my Granny came to the bus station to visit us, and I was centimetre

Teacher: Jones, what is the outside of a tree called?
Jones: I don't know, sir.
Teacher: Bark, boy, bark!
Jones: Woof woof!

The Completely Misleading Guide to School,
Jim Eldridge

Why Are Fire Engines Red?

In English, riddles are usually quite short, and are found largely in children's games and conversation.

What has two legs and flies? A pair of trousers.

But longer riddles can be found. 'Why are fire engines red?', in one version, has a twelve-line response:

One and one are two.
Two and two are four.
Three times four is twelve.
There are twelve inches in a ruler.
Queen Mary was a ruler.
Queen Mary ruled the sea.
There are fish in the sea.
The fish have fins.
The Finns fought the Russians.
The Russians are red.
Fire engines are always rushin'.
That's why fire engines are red.

The English Language,
David Crystal

Babies for Free

In the early days of American films, cinemas used to try all kinds of publicity stunts to fool their customers into coming to see a film. One favourite was to announce in the local paper that to celebrate the opening of a new film, the cinema's owners would give a baby away. This, as you can imagine, provoked a howl of protest. Mothers and fathers wrote in from all around complaining that it was cruel and stirring up a great debate. The cinema owner would say that as the mother of the baby didn't mind it being given away, and as the baby itself didn't have any complaints, they didn't understand what was wrong.

More outrage and more letters to the newspaper followed, and on the day the cinema would be packed out with people waiting to see what happened. When they found that the owner was giving away a baby pig or dog, they were all very embarrassed at being so easily caught out.

My Most Embarrassing Moment

School jokes

1 What do these three jokes have in common?

2 Do you know any more jokes like this? If you do, share them with the rest of your group.

Why are fire engines red?

1 Which words in the riddle have the same sounds, but different meanings?

2 There are a lot of words like this, e.g. cell/sell, male/mail, wait/weight, sail/sale. How many more can you think of? Make a list of them.

3 Use your list to help you to write a riddle like the one about fire engines. You might start it like this:

The ship sailed on the sea.
C comes after B.
Bees make honeycombs...

Try to think of a way of linking your first line with your last.

4 Research some jokes and riddles and rehearse them. Perform them for your group or class. Record your performance on cassette or video.

Babies for free

1 What is a 'publicity stunt'?

2 Why were some cinema-goers 'caught out'?

Mixed-up School

We have a crazy mixed-up school.
Our teacher Mrs Cheetah
Makes us talk backwards. Nicer cat
You wouldn't want to meet a.

To start the day we eat our lunch,
Then do some heavy dome-work.
The boys' and girls' rooms go to us,
The hamster marks our homework.

At recess time we race inside
To put on diving goggles,
Play pin-the-donkey-on-the-tail,
Ball-foot or ap-for-bobbles.

Old Cheetah, with a chunk of chalk,
Writes right across two blackbirds,
And when she says, 'Go home!' we walk
The whole way barefoot backwards.

X. J. Kennedy

Here are the Football Results

League Division Fun
Manchester United won, Manchester City lost.
Crystal Palace 2, Buckingham Palace 1
Millwall Leeds nowhere
Wolves 8 A cheese roll and had a cup of tea 2
Aldershot 3 Buffalo Bill shot 2
Evertonill, Liverpool's not very well either
Newcastle's Heaven Sunderland's a very nice place 2
Ipswich one? You tell me.

Michael Rosen

Unusual Shoelaces

To lace my shoes
I use spaghetti.
Teacher and friends
All think I'm batty.

Let 'em laugh, the whole
Kit and kaboodle.
I'll get by.
I use my noodle.

X. J. Kennedy

We Doubt It

Little boy: I et four eggs for breakfast this morning.
Big sister: You mean ate.
Little boy: Maybe you're right. Maybe I et eight eggs for breakfast this morning!

Jokes, Quotes and One-liners for Public Speakers

Mixed-up school

You are a pupil in Mrs Cheetah's school. Describe your favourite lesson, in which everything happens 'wardbacks' (backwards!).

Unusual shoelaces

1 Make a list of some everyday objects that might have unusual uses, e.g. spaghetti as shoelaces, wellingtons as a vase, GPO post box as a nesting box, hard-boiled egg as a golf ball.

2 Use this list to help you to write a letter to a friend about a strange hotel you stayed at. It might start like this:

Dear....
You'll never guess what happened to me last week when I was staying at...

Here are the football results

Michael Rosen's poem includes many words which sound like other words, e.g. 'won' sounds like 'one', and '8' sounds like 'ate'. The humour in the poem depends on these words. Can you find any other words in the poem that are used in this way?

Ed McLachlan

Cartoons

Draw some more cartoons using these words:

- sloping • cracked • bent
- do not fold • reflection
- heavy • light

Or choose some words or phrases of your own to illustrate instead.

There You Are

The Spoken Word,
Richard McRoberts

Travel Games

Alphabet Tales

This is an alphabetical game, but it doesn't involve any writing. The aim is to tell a story from player to player going right through the alphabet.

Player Number One thinks of a subject for the story beginning with an A. For example, he might say: 'A was an artichoke'. The second player carries the tale on by naming an incident beginning with B: 'B baked it'. On it goes: 'C cooked it', 'D diced it', 'E encrusted it', 'F fried it', 'G gobbled it all up' – until (if you're all clever enough) you get to Z...

...Any player who fails to think up a suitable incident within a short time-limit (say, five seconds) must drop out. If nobody has won by the time you reach Z, then you begin again at A.

Hidden Animals

How do you hide a hippo in a sentence? It's easy. All you have to do is split up the word and disguise the pieces by fitting them into other words. See if you can find 'hippo' in this sentence.

'He dined off fish and chip potatoes.'

The 'hip' of 'chip' plus the 'po' of 'potatoes' makes 'hippo'. Likewise the sentence 'How tall a man is he?' contains the word 'llama', and 'Stop and ask the way' contains the word 'panda'.

Try hiding an animal yourself, and see if the other passengers can guess what it is. If you find it difficult working out these posers in your head, then write them down on a sheet of paper.

This game can also be played with towns, colours, countries, peoples' names or any other suitable topic.

Children's Travel Games,
Andrew Langley

There you are

1 The phrase 'There you are' can be said in a number of ways, to give a number of different meanings. What does the phrase mean in each picture?

2 How many different ways can these phrases be said?

- What are you doing here?
- Nobody wants you to speak!
- Do you know the number?

Drawing some simple cartoons may help you to illustrate the different meanings each phrase can have.

Travel games

1 Try playing Alphabet Tales with 2 or 3 people in your group. Keep a record of the letters which are easy or hard to use. What makes a letter easy or hard to use? A dictionary will help you answer this question.

2 Make up sentences which contain these 'hidden' foods:
• bread • meat • pear
• egg • fish • ham

3 Write down the rules of a 'travel' game you have played on a journey. Teach the game to your teacher or others in your group.

Snodding

When I broke a window
And my father said,
'Are you sure you didn't do it?'
I just snodded my head.
'Are you with us or against us?'
The school bully asked.
I snodded my head
Until the danger passed.
When I tell a lie
I turn bright red,
But I feel much safer
If I only snod my head.

Gargling with Jelly,
Brian Patten

I've Lost My Car!

'I've lost my car, I've lost my car,
It's nowhere to be seen!
I've lost my car, I've lost my car,
And it was red and green!'

'I've found your car, I've found your car,
Outside the barber's shop!
I've found your car, I've found your car,
I am a clever cop!'

'A clever cop? Don't make me laugh,
You've no brains in your head!
The car I lost was red and green,
That car is green and red!'

Colin West

Changing His Mind

'Yes means no
and no means yes,'
said my brother
on the way to the park,
making conversation.

Mum gave us bread
for the ducks
but he said no,
he wouldn't feed them
and no to sailing boats,

and no to skimming stones
across the water,
no to the roundabout
the swings and slide,

but he cried
when he didn't get an ice-cream.
'Yes means yes
and no means no,'
said my brother.

Ask a Silly Question,
Irene Rawnsley

Snodding

1 What is a 'snod'?

2 Write a list of 'in-between' words, like 'snod', and their meanings, e.g. cry and laugh gives you 'craugh'.
Compare your list with those of others in your class or group.

3 Arrange all the words in alphabetical order to make a mini-dictionary. Writing each word on a slip of paper will make it easier to organize the words into alphabetical order. Check (using a large dictionary) that none of the invented words in your mini-dictionary are real words. If they are, then add these real meanings to your invented definitions.

4 Use some of your invented words in a poem or story.

I've lost my car

Write a story about someone who loses their black and white *cat*. A neighbour finds it, but the cat owner makes the same silly mistake as the car owner. You should be able to work out what the last line of your story will be. The poem gives you a big clue.

Changing his mind

Young children often play this sort of game: turning 'yes' into 'no', or 'up' into 'down'. Can you remember playing these sorts of word games when you were younger? Write down the names of the word games you used to play and discuss them with a partner.

Broken Plate

The Spoken Word,
Richard McRoberts

Bickering

One of Sid's pleasures was to charge at the girls playing hopscotch on the pavement and kick away the stone that they pushed seriously one-legged from hell to heaven. When they saw him coming the girls ran away shrieking and from a safe distance called him nasty names and poked their tongues out at him. One afternoon a tall, fair girl didn't run away, but waited for him truculently. They met in the middle of the chalked oblong and there was a tussle. Sid got the stone and, wide trouser legs flapping, started to dribble it along the road. The girl ran after him, furiously scooping up dirt and pebbles from the gutter and hurling them at his back. Sid could run and dribble well, but he wasn't a bully, so he stopped to let the girl catch up with him.

'Say you're sorry,' the girl demanded.

'You're sorry,' Sid said.

'Say you're sorry.'

'You're sorry.'

The girl stamped her foot.

'Say... you're... sorry.'

'I have said it,' Sid sputtered.

'No you haven't.'

'Yes I have.'

'No you haven't!'

'You said say you're sorry and I said you're sorry. Didn't I?' Sid turned to me with an aggrieved expression.

'Didn't I?' he repeated appealingly.

'Yes,' I said, 'you did.'

The Railway Game,
Clifford Dyment

Broken plate

1 What do you think the same people in the cartoon would have said to the little girl if she came into the house soaking wet?

2 What do you think the same people would say to an *adult* who turns up late for an appointment?

Bickering

1 Why was the girl so furious with Sid?

2 The girls 'shrieked' at Sid and 'called him nasty names and poked their tongues out at him'. Is this an accurate picture of how girls react in this kind of situation?

3 How do you think the group of boys would have reacted if the tall, fair girl had disrupted *their* game?

4 Write 6 to 8 sentences about the main differences between the ways 11 to 12 year-old girls and boys play in the schoolyard or field.

Me, Myself, I

God Made the Rivers

God made the rivers,
God made the lakes,
God made you.
We all make mistakes.

Autograph verse

How I See It

Some say the world's
A hopeless case:
A speck of dust
In all that space.
It's certainly
A scruffy place.
Just one hope
For all the human race
That I can see:
Me. I'm
ACE!

Hot Dog,
Kit Wright

Tales Out of School

I remember in my last year at primary school the teacher tended to arrange the desks so that the people doing best were near the front, going back to the ones who weren't doing very well, which I thought was a bit bad. It made you think you had to get on to the next desk and you got all upset about it. I was in the middle.

I never really thought about things. You're not mature enough to take any notice. You just go along with it.

Ley Alberici, aged 17,
Great Barr, Birmingham, 1983

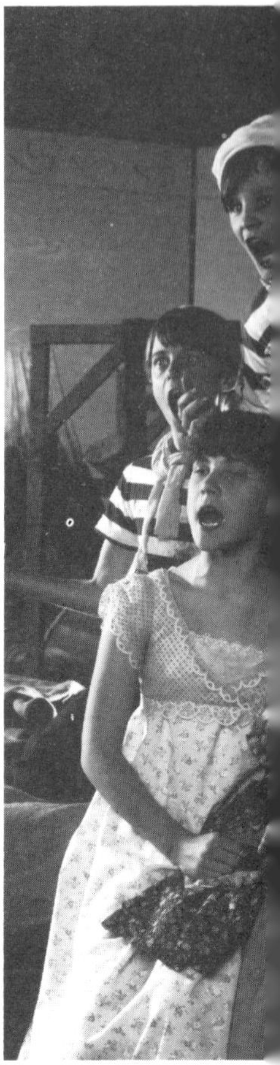

The Hidden Talent

In Rain
Her shoes like ship-wrecks, water seeping in,
Pull at the torn rigging of her tights.

In Class,
The blackboard an illusion, worlds away,
That with a bell fades gently into mist.

In Goal
The ball flies past her to the greedy net,
She stands there, in amazement at the cries.

On Stage,
She weaves a web of talent-laden silk
Her listeners hanging on her words like flies.

Ailie Donald

God made the rivers

How is this poem different from 'How I See It' and 'The Hidden Talent'?

How I see it

1 Is it wrong to brag? Is it conceited (big-headed) to talk about your good points and your achievements?

2 Write a poem about yourself that ends with the line 'Me? I'm ACE!'.

Tales out of school

1 How did Ley feel about the way his primary schoolteacher arranged the desks?

2 What do you think would be the best way to arrange desks in a primary classroom?

3 What can primary schoolteachers do to build confidence in young learners?

4 Can teachers of older students use the same approaches?

The hidden talent

1 What was the girl's 'hidden talent'?

2 Lots of people have hidden talents. Do you know anyone like the girl in the poem?

3 What are your hidden talents? Write a short pen portrait of yourself in 8 to 10 sentences. Stress your good points!

4 What sorts of talents do the young people in these two photos have? Collect some similar photos and use them to create a collage entitled: 'We Can Do Anything!'. Stick speech balloons onto your collage to show what the young people in each photo are thinking.

Shadows

Chunks of night
Melt
In the morning sun.
One lonely one
Grows legs
And follows me
To school.

Patricia Hubbell

Treasure Trove

I have a tin
to keep things in
underneath
my bedroom floor.

I put my finger
in the crack,
quietly lift
the floor-board back,

and there's my store,
safely hid
in a tin with roses
on the lid.

A few feathers
and a chicken's claw,
a big tooth
from a dinosaur,

the wrapper
from my Easter egg,
a Christmas robin
with one leg,

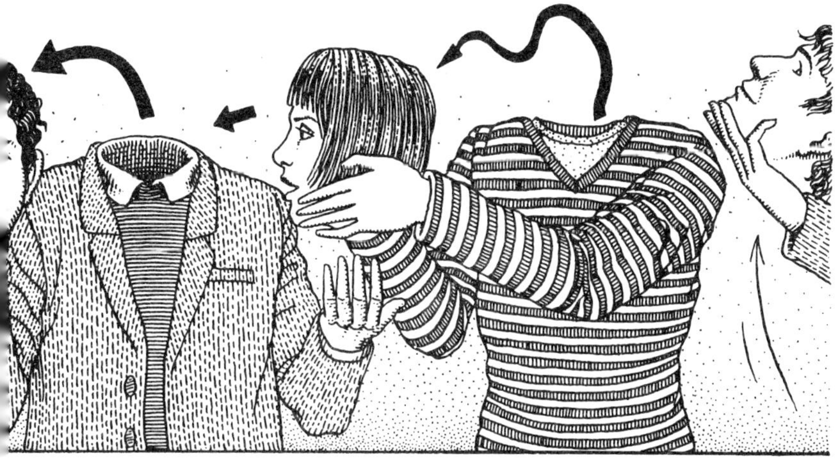

long hairs
from a horse's mane,
real pesetas
come from Spain,

three of my
operation stitches,
like spiders
wrapped in bandages,

a marble
full of dragon smoke,
flashing with fire
in the dark,

a magic pebble
round and white,
a sparkler left
from bonfire night.

Underneath
my bedroom floor
there's a treasure tin,
with my things in.

Ask a Silly Question,
Irene Rawnsley

Changing heads

1 What would it be like to 'change heads' for a day? You would experience someone else's thoughts, feelings and memories.
If you were asked to take part in a 'head swapping' experiment, would you?

2 Which famous people would/wouldn't you like to swap heads with and why?

Shadows

Describe a day in your life, seen through the eyes of your shadow. How does it feel, having to follow you about all day and every day? Try to think of your shadow as a person. Give it a name and a personality. What are the good and the bad sides of its character?

Treasure trove

1 When we are young, certain small things, e.g. a teddy, a marble or a feather, often have great value for us. Ask other people in your group what sorts of things they treasured when they were younger.

2 Write a short autobiographical story about one particular object that had special importance for you as a child. Say how you got the object. Describe it in detail and say why it became 'special'.
If you still have the object, compare how it looks now with what it looked like when you first got it.

Evacuated

I have this image of a small boy with a label tied round his neck. The boy has no features and is crying. He is carrying a cardboard box, which contains his gasmask.

I remember that labels with our names on were pinned to our clothes before we left London. I think I felt that I had no identity and was a parcel being posted to the country. The labels frightened me as much as the idea of leaving my parents. A child of seven, if lost, can tell people his name. A label assumes that he does not know his name, or worse, has no name and is given one at random from a list of names.

Perhaps the gasmask felt like a second face, a mask that would replace my own face as soon as I left London. I remember that the gasmask looked inhuman with its celluloid eyeshield and metal snout. I remember that it smelt of rubber and that I could not breathe properly inside it. The shield misted over with condensation and it felt warm and suffocating inside this second face.

The Rebel

When everybody has short hair,
The rebel lets his hair grow long.

When everybody has long hair,
The rebel cuts his hair short.

When everybody talks during the lesson,
The rebel doesn't say a word.

When nobody talks during the lesson,
The rebel creates a disturbance.

When everybody wears a uniform,
The rebel dresses in fantastic clothes.

When everybody wears fantastic clothes,
The rebel dresses soberly.

In the company of dog lovers,
The rebel expresses a preference for cats.

In the company of cat lovers,
The rebel puts in a good word for dogs.

When everybody is praising the sun,
The rebel remarks on the need for rain.

When everybody is greeting the rain,
The rebel regrets the absence of sun.

When everybody goes to the meeting,
The rebel stays at home and reads a book.

When everybody stays at home and reads a book.
The rebel goes to the meeting.

When everybody says, Yes please,
The rebel says, No thank you.

When everybody says, No thank you,
The rebel says, Yes please.

It is very good that we have rebels,
You may not find it very good to be one.

D. J. Enright

I know that we rehearsed the evacuation every morning for a week. Each morning my sister and I would leave home with our packed sandwiches and clothes. We would say goodbye to our parents. Our labels were pinned on and I felt sick.

Mel Calman

Evacuated

1 Interview 2 or 3 senior citizens about the Second World War. They may have been evacuated themselves.
Prepare well for the interview. Have a list of questions ready. Try to ask open questions, e.g. 'What did you like most dislike about...?'.
The people you speak to may let you tape the interview. If so, check the tape recorder beforehand. If not, you will need to make notes on their comments. Aim for a short, well-planned interview lasting 5-10 minutes.

2 Use your notes or tape to write a short account of the interview. Compare Mel Calman's experiences of the war with those of the senior citizens you talked to. Remember, the people you interview will be interested to read what you have written about them.

The rebel

1 Do you think it is 'good that we have rebels'?

2 What makes a person a rebel?

3 Would you describe yourself as a rebel?

4 You live next door to a family of rebels. Describe them, their home, their life-style. Start by making up a short pen portrait of each member of this family. You will have to invent names, ages, etc. These pen portraits could be organized like the one shown on the left.

Mum and Dad and Me

I knocked a vase of flowers
over Dad's chair
the other day;
he was sitting there
at the time.

'Just look at me,' he shouted,
'I'm wet!
I'll skin you alive, my lad
Get upstairs to bed,
no arguing!

But Mum calmed him down,
mopped him up,
made a fresh brew,
said, 'If your son's clumsy
he takes after you.'

Today I painted those flowers,
purple and red;
the teacher said
I could bring my picture home.
Mum was pleased.

'If I were you I would
pin it up for Dad to see.
You're very good
at painting, my lad,
you take after me!'

Ask a Silly Question,
Irene Rawnsley

Crayfish and Tomato

I was allowed certain privileges now I was at school. The best one was being allowed to stay up later than the others and share Dad's tea. He loved seafood. He had a drinking mate with a boat, and if there was a good catch, crayfish came our way. Fleshy, white crayfish and tomato dipped in vinegar, that was Dad's favourite meal. At first, I hated the taste of vinegar, but I gradually grew accustomed to it. I was careful not to eat a lot, I knew how much Dad enjoyed crays. It was a happy time then, crays and tomato, Dad and me.

We had some good times, then. Some nights, Dad would hide chocolates in the deep pockets of his overalls and we were allowed to fish them out. Sometimes, he'd laugh and joke, and when he swore, we knew he didn't really mean it.

Dad slipped in and out of our lives. He was often in hospital for periods of a few days to a month or so, and the longest he was at home at one time was about three months; usually, it was a lot less. When he first came home from hospital, he would be so doped up with drugs he wasn't able to communicate much... Every time he returned from hospital, he had to try and find another job. Mum provided the only steady income, with various part-time jobs, mostly cleaning.

When Dad was happy, I wished he'd never change. I wanted him to be like that for ever, but there was always the war. Just when things seemed to be looking up, it would intrude and overwhelm us. The war had never ended for Dad. He lived with it day and night.

My Place,
Sally Morgan

Mum and dad and me

1 In what way is the boy supposed to take after his father?

2 In what way is he supposed to take after his mother?

3 Think of your own personality and abilities. In what ways are you like your parents?

4 Do you think girls grow up to be more like their mothers, and boys like their fathers?

5 What qualities do you have that you hope your children will have too?

Crayfish and tomato

1 Sally is looking back on the relationship she had with her father when she was 6 years old. What did she like about her father then?

2 How did the war affect her father and Sally's relationship with him?

3 Young people often see their parents differently as they grow up. How do you think Sally's view of her father might have changed as she got older?

4 Write a story about a young person whose feelings towards an adult relative change dramatically as they grow up. This change of mind might come about because the two people get to know each other better in a crisis, for example. Or they may discover they share an interest in the same hobby.

Not Me!

Every little girl would like to be
the fairy on the Christmas tree
except me.
I'd rather be
a Kung-Fu fighter like Bruce Lee.

Every little girl would like to be
The Queen of the May
and reign for a day.
I'd rather stow away
and hitch-hike across the USA.

Every little girl would like to be
a bridesmaid or a bride;
not me. I'd rather ride
a motorbike. Or hide
inside a pirate's cave. Or save
a penalty-kick at Wembley.
Or have the Secret Service send me
on missions as a spy. Or fly
a shuttle into space. Or race
against Sebastian Coe. I know
what other little girls would like to be

Not me!

The Phantom Lollipop Lady,
Adrian Henri

Family Dinner

A family settled down for dinner at a restaurant. The waitress first took the order of the adults, then turned to the seven-year-old.

'What will you have?' she asked.

The boy looked around the table timidly and said, 'I would like to have a hot dog.'

Before the waitress could write down the order, the mother interrupted. 'No hot dogs,' she said. 'Get him a steak with mashed potatoes and carrots.'

The waitress ignored her. 'Do you want ketchup or mustard on your hot

dog?' she asked the boy.

'Ketchup.'

'Coming up in a minute,' said the waitress as she started for the kitchen.

There was a stunned silence when she left. Finally the boy looked at everyone present and said, 'Know what? She thinks I'm real!'

The Heart of Enlightenment,
Anthony de Mello

Parents and Teenagers,
Health Education Council

Not me!

1 Talk to 5 or 6 people in your group. Ask them about their childhood, their hobbies, their likes and dislikes. Try to find out 2 or 3 things about each person that surprise you. Make a list of these 'surprises'.

2 Write a sentence about each person like this:

I was surprised to learn that Jane... because...

3 Write a story or a poem about a new pupil who joins your group. At first you think the new pupil is very boring. But as you get to know them you get a big surprise!

Family dinner

1 What does the boy mean when he says, 'She thinks I'm real?'

2 What does the story tell you about the waitress?

3 What does it tell you about the parents?

4 Have you ever found yourself in this sort of situation? If so, how did you react?

5 Can you see any links between 'Family Dinner' and the cartoon?

6 Use the story to write a conversation between the boy in the restaurant and his best friend. Start it like this:

Boy: You'll never guess what happened last night.
Friend: What?
Boy: We went out for a meal and...

A Sporting Chance

Games

I hate games
When the cold November wind
Freezes your knees,
White and knocking,
And the mud squirts
Up your shorts
When some fat show-off
Flattens you in rugby.
Or they make you
Struggle up treadmill hills
In something called cross-country,
But which is really
Cross slag-heap
(Made into a park
Now used as a dogs' toilet.)
And even rain
Brings no release:
It's into the dusty sports hall
Chasing a huge orange basket ball
You never touch
And being bumped and battered
In a no-contact game
(The teacher says.)
On such days
The happiest sound
Is the drawn out squeal
Of the final whistle.

John Price

In netball the players wear lettered vests to indicate their positions, so that the umpire knows if they are in the wrong area.

Basketball

In 1891 some young Americans wanted a game they could play indoors. They hung peach baskets on the walls at opposite ends of a gymnasium and two teams tried to score points by throwing a large ball into the baskets.

Basketball has now become a very popular game throughout the world. The number of players is now five on each team, and the basket has been replaced by a metal hoop and net. No physical contact is allowed, and the ball can only be passed or bounced (dribbled) around the court. The defending side wins the ball either by intercepting it or as a result of a foul by their opponents. Two points are usually scored for a basket, and the team with the most points wins the game.

Netball

This is a team game with seven players a side. Netball is played mainly by girls and women, although it is increasingly popular among men. It is played on a hard court, usually out of doors, and the aim is to score goals by throwing the ball up into the opposition's net, which is placed about 3 metres (10 feet) above the ground.

Each player has a named position and is restricted to a particular area of the court. Running with the ball is not allowed, and so all progress forward is made by passing the ball hand to hand until it reaches the goal shooter or goal attack, who are the only people allowed to shoot at the net and score.

In volleyball players have to jump high to smash the ball downwards.

Volleyball

This is a game for six players a side. Each team tries to hit or knock the ball with hand or arm (or any part of the body above the waist) over the net so that the opposing team is unable to return it or prevent it from hitting the ground.

Each team can hit the ball a maximum of three times before sending it back across the net, but they cannot catch or hold the ball.

The game was invented in 1895 in America by a games instructor called William Morgan. He wanted a game for people who did not want to play basketball.

Oxford Children's Encyclopedia

Games

1 Do a survey of your group (or a group of a similar age) to find out what they feel about games. Try to ask about 10 to 12 people. Set out your findings in a chart like this:

Name	What do you dislike about games?	What do you like?
Jon	*Getting changed in cold changing rooms...*	*Being part of a team*

2 The BBC are coming to your school to make a film about school games. You are one of the pupils they would like to interview. You will be expected to talk about how you feel about games. But you will also be expected to talk about how others (boys and girls) feel about it too.
Use the chart of results from your survey to write down what you would say during an interview. Try to make general as well as personal comments.

e.g. *I like games because .... but a few of my friends think ....*

Basketball, Netball and Volleyball

1 In what ways are the three sports the same?

2 In what ways are they different?

3 You have been asked to write a short entry in a new junior encylopedia of sports. The entry must be no longer than 60 words but must contain the most important information about one sport. Write an entry for a sport you are interested in.

Fancy Dive

The fanciest dive that ever was dove
Was done by Melissa of Coconut Grove
She bounced on the board and flew into the air
With a twist of her head and a twirl of her hair.
She did thirty-four jackknives, backflipped and spun,
Quadruple gainered, and reached for the sun,
And then somersaulted nine times and a quarter –
And looked down and saw that the pool had no water.

Shel Silverstein

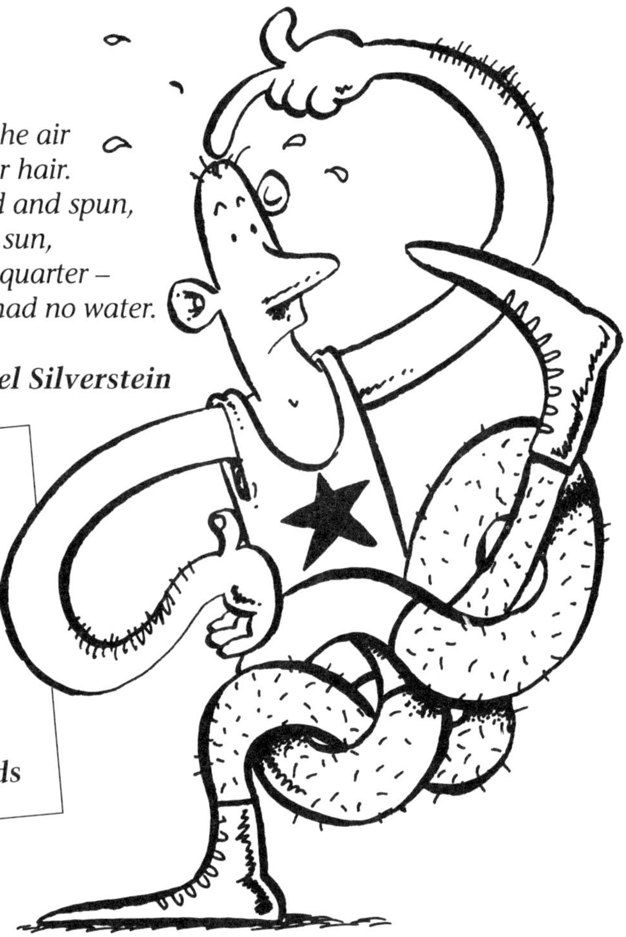

The Wrestler's Complaint

A wrestler said: 'I'm in a spot!
The pace is becoming too hot!
My opponent's unfair –
He's pulled out my hair,
And tied both my legs in a knot.'

Frank Richards

American Football

American football is more like rugby than soccer, with a similar oval ball, H-shaped posts, and a similar method of scoring. A touchdown (six points) is scored by getting the ball into the area behind the goal-line, the end zone. An extra point is scored by then kicking the ball between the posts and over the bar. A field goal is worth three points.

As in rugby, handling is permitted. Players make progress by running with the ball or passing the ball by hand. Unlike rugby, you can pass the ball forward and defenders can block players who do not have the ball. It is also a game of constant stops and starts. Teams are given four attempts at 'downs' to move the ball ten yards, hence the markings on the pitch. Teams have 40 players, with eleven on the field at one time.

The game is played professionally in the USA and Canada. College football, the home of the game, has some different rules. Canadian football too is a bit different. There are twelve players on a bigger pitch.

Oxford Children's Encyclopedia

Fancy dive

1 Have you ever tried to do a trick or stunt and got it horribly wrong?

2 Make a list of things that might go wrong in a variety of sports or hobbies:

e.g. a pole vaulter's pole might snap
a polo player might knock themselves out with a polo stick

3 Write a description (like the one of Melissa's dive) about a sports person who tries a stunt, but gets it spectacularly wrong.
Try to build up the action as much as you can by giving plenty of details of the stunt, the crowd, the stadium, etc.

Here are some of the helmets worn by teams in the American National Football League to protect them from injury.

The wrestler's complaint

1 Wrestlers often have 'stage names' like Harry 'The Haystack' Hogan, Mike 'The Masked Mauler' Mason, Brenda 'Barndoor' Boston.
Invent some 'stage names' for these wrestlers: Bob Little, Connie Holland, Rob Falcon, Lesley Cookson. Their stage names should give a clue about the size and weight of the fighter and any special tricks or moves they use.

2 Write a report of a wrestling match to go with this headline:

It's KNOT a laughing matter.

Who was fighting? What happened during the match? Who won?

American football

1 What are the main differences between American football and soccer?

2 If you and a group of friends got together to form an American football team, what team name would you use?

3 Design a strip, including a helmet, for your team. Decide on the logo that you will put on your strip.
It should go with your team name.

Keeping Fit

Vigorous exercise is important throughout life, but especially so while you are still developing. It is essential for:

1 **Strength** Muscles actually waste away if they are not used. Vigorous exercise increases their size and builds up their strength.

2 **Suppleness** If joints are not regularly stretched to their full extent, they stiffen. Exercise will help you move with grace and ease.

3 **Stamina** Muscles need to keep on going, not collapse after one quick burst of effort. You build up physical stamina by regular exercise.

4 **Safety** Vigorous exercise gets rid of tense, anxious, or angry feelings. You feel pleasantly tired, more relaxed about problems, and less likely to be upset.

Athletic ability

Some people are naturally athletic... Others have to work hard... This is the way people are – naturally different. But it would be a mistake to give up exercise just because you are not naturally athletic.

Different skills

...There are different kinds of exercise to suit people's different body skills and personalities. If you dislike competitive sports, have you thought of jogging or cycling, swimming or rowing, dancing or aerobics, or simply exercising in the privacy of your room?

***All About Health*,**
Dorothy Baldwin

How to Get Out of Games

An illness or some sort of injury is the obvious first choice here.

You could try sneezing a lot and saying, 'Please Sir/Miss, I think I've got flu.'

Unfortunately most teachers are so hard-hearted they couldn't care less if you've got bubonic plague. They just say, 'Get out on that field. The fresh air will do you good.'

However, here is a list of illnesses which you can try to persuade your teacher you are suffering from:

- rheumatism
- typhoid
- a common cold
- malaria
- swamp fever
- a swollen head
- tennis elbow
- housemaid's knee
- Yeti's toenails
- Frankenstein's foot
- lumbago

The Completely Misleading Guide to School,
Jim Eldridge

Keeping fit

1 Person **A** likes to do a lot of healthy exercise. Person **B** hates it. Write a short dialogue between **A** and **B** in which **A** tries to persuade **B** to be more active. Use information from 'Keeping Fit' to support **A**'s argument.

2 What other kinds of exercise could you do if you do not like competitive sports?

Volleyball cartoon

1 What is the idea behind the cartoon?

2 Some people believe that there is no point in playing a game 'unless you play to win'. For them, winning is all that matters; winning at all costs. How important is winning to you?

How to get out of games

1 Make your own list of 10 'way out' illnesses or injuries that might be used as an excuse for missing games.

2 Use one of these illnesses or injuries in a note to a P.E. teacher, explaining why your daughter or son cannot do games.

3 Read this note to a partner in your group or class. Ask your partner to imagine they are the P.E. teacher. Ask them to write a reply to your note. You do the same for your partner.
Do not be rude or aggressive in your reply, e.g.

'You must think I'm an idiot if you expect me to believe a 20 metre white shark attacked your precious son...'

Try to be tactful, e.g.

'Thank you for your note. I was amazed to read about the shark...'

I'm Panting

Why talk
when you can shout.
Why walk
when you can run.
Why just live
when you can blaze like fire.

I'm running and shouting with joy,
I'm running and shouting with grief.
I'm panting,
my lungs are working like mad.

Violent feelings
are supposed to be good for you.

Fat Like the Sun,
Anna Swir

Biking

Fingers grip,
toes curl;
head down,
wheels whirl.

Hair streams,
fields race;
ears sting,
winds chase.

Breathe deep,
troubles gone;
just feel
windsong.

Midnight Forest,
Judith Evans

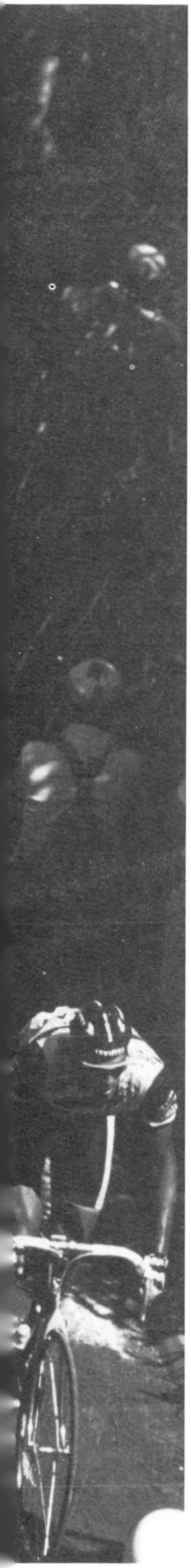

Hunker Hawser

This game is sure to prove that 'the harder they come, the harder they fall'. If you like one-on-one competition, here it is – along with a real surprise as to what gets you off your pedestal.

Pedestals are about 6 inches high and small enough so that players can't move their feet without losing balance. (A good mount might be a block of wood or styrofoam, a tree stump, or try an overturned pot of the cooking, flower, chimney, or even chamber variety.)

Players hunker down on their platforms, which are set about 6 feet apart, each holding one end of a rope about one inch in diameter and at least 15 feet long. The excess rope lies coiled between them – but not for long.

At the starting signal, the players begin reeling in. The object is to unbalance your opponent by tightening or slackening the rope. Sound simple? 'Oh I'll just give a good pull and...' Suddenly your opponent relaxes her hold, and over you go in a spectacular backward somersault – defeated by your own energy. In fact, the more aggressive you become, the more vulnerable you are. The whole idea of how to win becomes as topsy-turvy in this game as the chamber pot on which you're standing.

We've been hankering to know what Hunker Hawser would be like with 3 people and a Y-shaped rope. Or lots of hunkerers and a circular rope.

***The New Games Book*,**
ed. Andrew Fleugelman

I'm panting

1 Is it healthy to let off steam now and then? Or should feelings be kept under control?
Are 'violent feelings' good for you? What do you and your friends do when you want to 'blaze like fire'?

2 In certain sports, (e.g. volleyball, ice hockey) we see people 'blaze like fire'. In other sports competitors are much calmer. 'Keeping Fit' (on page 42) claims that exercise helps you to get rid of 'tense and angry feelings'. Do you agree/disagree with this? Give your reasons.

Hunker Hawser

1 What sort of people will make good 'Hunker Hawser' players?

2 Why do you think it says 'the more aggressive you become, the more vulnerable you are'?

Gymnastics

Gymnastics was one of the nine original sports of the first modern Olympic Games in 1896. Its beginnings go back to the times of the ancient Greeks and Romans, whose young men used gymnastic exercises to become fit soldiers. The sport reached its present form in the early 1950s as a combination of two kinds of gymnastics pioneered in the last century, German and Swedish. The German system used apparatus which needed stength, while the Swedish method depended more on free exercises without equipment. The sport today demands from all gymnasts qualities such as concentration, daring, timing and balance.

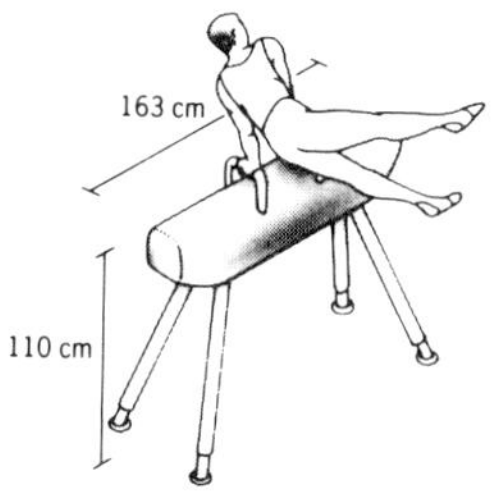

Pommel Horse The pommel horse, for men, is very difficult to master. Gymnasts must support their weight with one or both hands on the pommels (handles), or any other part of the horse, while they carry out circular movements with their legs.

Rings The rings require the most strength from men gymnasts, particularly in the arms and shoulders. The gymnast must also keep the rings from swinging when he performs handstands or swinging movements, so good timing is essential.

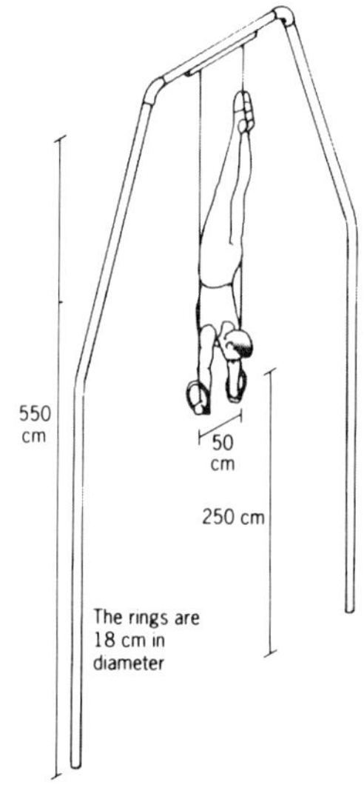

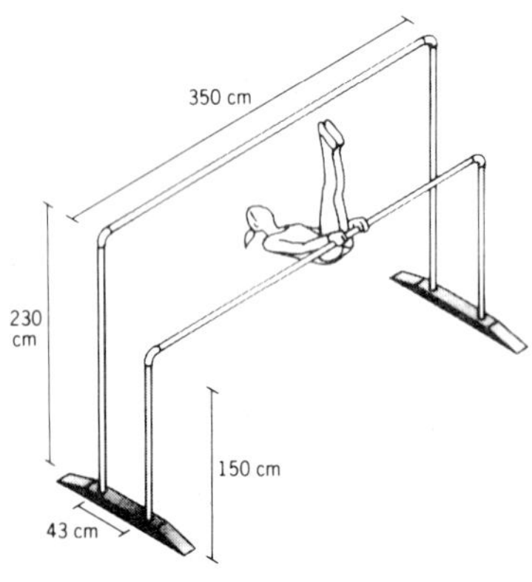

Asymmetric bars Adapted for women from the parallel bars, the asymmetric (uneven) bars require routines made up mostly of swinging movements from bar to bar. The exercise must flow without pausing or stopping, with changes in direction of movement.

Horizontal bar This is the most spectacular of the men's six exercises. Gymnasts have to perform continuous swinging movements without stopping. The movements must include circles, twists and changes of grasp. Performers can be more than 3 metres above the ground.

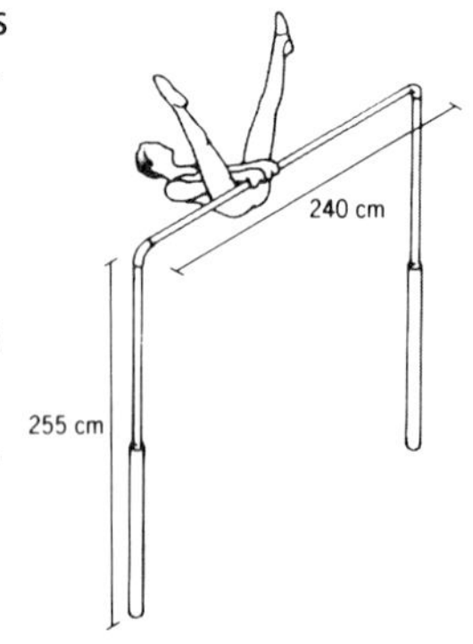

Training

Many of today's top gymnasts started training when they were very young. Boys perform on six pieces of apparatus, girls on four. But first, all gymnasts have to condition their bodies to acquire strength, suppleness and stamina. Helped by coaches, gymnasts undergo years of hard effort before they reach top-class standards.

Beam The beam is the only apparatus designed entirely for women. It features balance, as the gymnast must work on a narrow strip only 10 centimetres wide. Expert beam performers can execute many floor skills, such as back flips and somersaults.

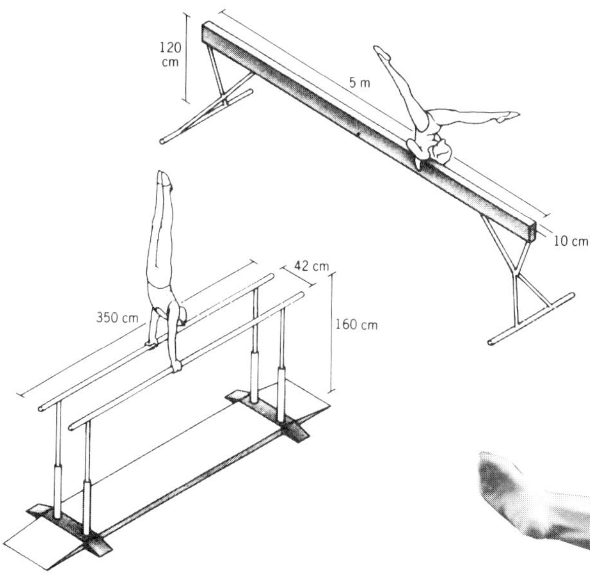

Parallel bars A parallel bars exercise calls for men gymnasts to produce handstands, turns, releases and re-grasps, and changes of direction as well as swinging and circling movements. The variety of skills required makes the piece popular.

Oxford Children's Encyclopedia

Gymnastics

1 Which of the gymnastic events illustrated do you think is the most dangerous?

2 Why do top gymnasts have to start training when they are very young?

3 You are a top Olympic gymnast. You are under a great deal of pressure to train, to keep up with your school work and to spend time with your friends and family. Describe how you cope with these pressures. What thoughts run through your mind as you practise hour after hour on the rings, beams and bars?
Try to get a rhythm into your writing to match the rhythm of your work-out in the gym. Use short sentences, 'sharp' words, repeated phrases (like a rap) to suggest energy and pace, and the feelings of success and achievement you get.

Home Sweet Home?

It Looked That Way

Bob: I think my mother wants to get rid of me.
Don: Why do you say that?
Bob: Well, this morning she wrapped my lunch in a road map.

Jokes, Quotes and One-liners for Public Speakers

Real Talent

Dad had some
talent

he could stand on
his head

he would make
that perfect tripod
then slowly
precisely
raise
his legs

then there he was

all six foot two
of him
upside down

smiling

Sheryl L. Nelms

The Evil Adults

We took the Evil Adults *in the middle of*
the night.
We swooped upon their houses
they came without a fight.
For we were many thousands and they
were twenty-two.
We walked them through the cheering
crowds
and locked them in the zoo.
Four of them were Teachers,
Six of them were Mums,
Eight of them were Fathers... stop
let me do my sums...
Two were Politicians,
Three were cruel and mean,
and one had just invented an anti-child
machine.

We put them in the Tiger cage,
The tigers didn't mind,
they ate the Evil Adults... *man and*
woman kind.
Grown-ups of this town be warned,
We are watching you,
Treat your children kindly,
Or you know what we will do.

Sue Townsend

It looked that way

What other 'hints' could Bob's mother have given him? Think up some more.
e.g. She could have rented his bedroom out to a lodger.

Evil adults

1 Sue Townsend includes teachers, parents and politicians in her list of 'evil adults'. Is she being fair? Who would you include in your list?

2 What do you think an 'anti-child machine' does?
Draw an anti-child machine and use the drawing in an advert. The advert might include phrases like:

'What every parent needs!'
'No home should be without one!'

You will need to invent details like price (inc. VAT), measurements, power source, insurance, guarantee, etc.
You might include testimonials, like this one, from satisfied customers.

Mrs Smith of Swindon says, 'I was amazed by the effect this machine had on my awful nephew...'

Rather Peculiar Pets

Mum was passionately interested in the world of nature, and avidly watched any television programme dealing with cruelty to animals. She would sit in her favourite chair by the fireside and, between sobs, decry the brutality of man. The fact that, while she did this, she was surrounded by a small, but growing, collection of glassy-eyed, taxidermied creatures never bothered her. Her passion was for the dead as well as the living.

One evening as she sat engrossed in a programme about the extinction of the Tasmanian tiger, I crept slowly around the darkened room. Mum failed to notice my movements, because she always insisted on watching television with the light turned off. She reckoned it made it more like the movies. By the time I returned to my own chair, I had managed to turn the faces of her entire collection towards her. When the Tasmanian tiger disappeared for good, Mum was feeling quite emotional. Consequently, when I suddenly turned on the light, pointed to the other occupants of the room and said, 'Mum, *look!*,' she completely broke down. The sight of all those glazed, accusing eyes was just too much, she fled to the kitchen.

After a good sob, she returned ready to berate me. By this time, I'd taken up residence in her fireside chair and was engrossed in a quiz show. She confronted me with, 'Sally, you sod of a kid, don't ever do that to...,' then, noticing that her entire collection was now standing in a small group, warming themselves by the fire, she paused in her tirade and asked, 'What are they doing there?'

'Poor things are cold,' I replied with a straight face. She was too big a woman not to see the humour of the situation. Between bursts of 'You're terrible,' she giggled uncontrollably.

My Place,
Sally Morgan

How to Talk to Your Mother

You are about to leave the house:
'Where are you going?'
'Out.'
'Out where?'
'Just out.'
'Who are you going with?'
'A friend.'
'Which friend?'
'Mom, just a friend, okay? Do you have to know everything?'
'I don't have to know everything. I just want to know who you're going out with.'
'Debby, okay?'
'Do I know Debby?'
'She's just a friend, okay?'
'Well, where are you going?'
'Out.'

You have just come home:
'Hi, Mom, did anyone call?'
'You did get one call, but I forgot to ask who it was.'
'Male or female?'
'Male.'
'And you didn't ask! Thanks, Mom, thanks a lot, I really appreciate it. For all I know it was the most important call of my life!'

You have just hung up the telephone:
'Who was that, dear?'
'Can't a person have some privacy once in a while!'

***Teenage Romance*,**
Delia Ephon

Rather peculiar pets

1 What are 'taxidermied creatures'?

2 What does 'extinction' mean?

3 Why did Sally's mother not notice what Sally was doing with the animals?

4 Why did Sally's mother run out of the room?

5 Write a story about Sally, her mother and the stuffed animals. You might start it with the arrival of an unusual new addition to the collection.

How to talk to your mother

1 Do mothers and/or fathers 'have to know everything'?

2 Do you find it easy to get privacy in your home?

3 Why do parents make rules about friends, times to be home by, etc.? What sort of rules would you have if you were the parent of teenage daughters or sons?

4 Talk to 5 or 6 other pupils in your group or class about privacy at home. Make some brief notes and use these to help you write a short article entitled 'Teenagers Need Space!'

What Parents Say

'I'm never there. When I am there, I'm tired. I feel I don't know them well enough, or they me. Patrick's just starting to talk now, and I don't understand – you know, just because I'm not with him enough. Mary has to tell me what it is he's saying, because she's with him all day and she understands his language.'

'I was fine when she was a baby. Not that I had much experience. But I felt I knew about mine, and I suppose because I was fairly confident, everything worked out. But it's got much more difficult now she's a toddler and demanding more and challenging me more... You know, some people say that they're no good with tiny babies but like it when they start to walk and talk. Well, with me it's the reverse. I think when she's older still, perhaps I'll be better than I am now.'

Why Sports Day Pupils Ran a Mile

The event thousands of school children secretly dread is racing towards them – school sports day.

But it's not the fear of losing the 400-metres relay that has them trembling in their trainers – it's the prospect of their parents coming last in the good taste stakes.

Mums who turn up looking like Madonna, or dads who arrive in flares and kipper ties will have their offspring sprinting the other way.

And mothers who, unlike sporty Princess Diana, finish last in the parents' races, could be in for the high jump with their youngsters.

According to shyness expert Dr Ray Crozier, of the University of Wales, some children can be permanently affected by their parents' behaviour in front of their school peers.

He has compiled a list of sports day gaffes for the competitive parent to avoid at all costs – although many may find them a tall order.

These include calling children by cringe-worthy pet names like Bunnykins or kissing and cuddling them in front of chums.

Bringing along little brothers or sisters, smoking and wearing clothes that are either too trendy (Mum) or not trendy

'I don't think I can explain it to you. I get mad at them, I complain about all the work, I worry over all the problems, I quite often get down, I'm almost always overtired... But at the same time, even when I'm going through the worst, I still know that I love them like... well, I can't tell you what that love feels like or what it's given me.'

The Parent Book,
Nancy Kohner

enough (Dad) could also be non-starters.

Turning up in tatty cars and coming last in parents' races will also fail to win any prizes.

Dr Crozier said yesterday: 'Children can end up feeling completely crushed at events like sports day – but the embarrassment is mainly off the field.

'Parents have to be careful not to spoil things – some children may not turn out very well.'

Today,
25 June 1991

What parents say

1 What do each of the mothers and the father think is the hardest thing about being a parent?

2 What qualities do you have that would make you a good parent?

3 Survey 10 to 12 students in your year. Ask them what they think makes a good parent. Record your results in a chart like this:

Name	Ideas on what makes a good parent
Ranjit	*Not really sure, lots of love, maybe?*

Sports day

1 What do parents do at sports day (and at other times when they visit school) that embarrasses their children?

2 Discuss this with others in your class or group. Make brief notes on the comments made and examples of embarrassment recalled. Use these notes to help you draw up a list of 'Dos and Don'ts for Parents Visiting School'.
You might set it out like this:

Dos and Don'ts for Parents Visiting School	
Do	Don't
Remember to come on the right day	*Come on your bike*

Seeing a Parent Cry for the First Time

I was only eight at the time and that morning my mother seemed quite happy and cheerful. I was all ready for school when my Dad came rushing in; he seemed in a terrible flap.

I said, 'Good-bye Mum.'

There was no answer, only a lot of muffled talk.

I said again, 'Good-bye Dad.'

There was still no answer so I walked out to catch the bus.

It was a long day and the classroom was stuffy. I couldn't work in the heat and I was glad when it was time to go home. When the bus got home, I went in and Mum and Dad weren't in. I changed and went to sit in the garden. It was too hot to play football with the lads and too hot to sit and play with dolls or go roller-skating with the girls, so I walked about.

When I got back home my Mum was sitting in the kitchen. She was looking miserable and very tired. I asked her what was wrong.

'Oh nothing. Your tea's on the table.'

'I know. I thought...'

'Well you know what thought did.'

'Oh well if you're in that sort of mood.'

I went to the table and started my tea. As I had just finished Dad walked in the door. He was pale and looked very ill.

'What's the matter Dad?' I said.

He walked straight past me as if he hadn't seen me.

I finished my tea and went out. I thought that was the best way.

After about half an hour I decided that I wanted to watch TV so I walked

Her Parents' Eyes

Linda Wade is very important to her mum and dad, both of whom have been blind since birth. By the time she was four in 1986, Linda was organizing shopping trips, guiding her parents in the street and even helping her mum put on make-up. At the supermarket Linda learnt to lead her mum to the right shelves and spot any bargains on offer. And when her parents had to travel by bus it was her responsibility to make sure they caught the right one.
But Linda was always surprised when people made a fuss of her and told her how wonderful she was. 'The only way I'm different from my friends is that I have to be much tidier', she said. 'I have to be careful not to leave things on the floor in case Mummy or Daddy trip over them.'

Front Page Kids,
Sarah Livinoff and Vida Adamoli

The young have a lot to learn from adults... teacher and pupil - what's today's lesson?

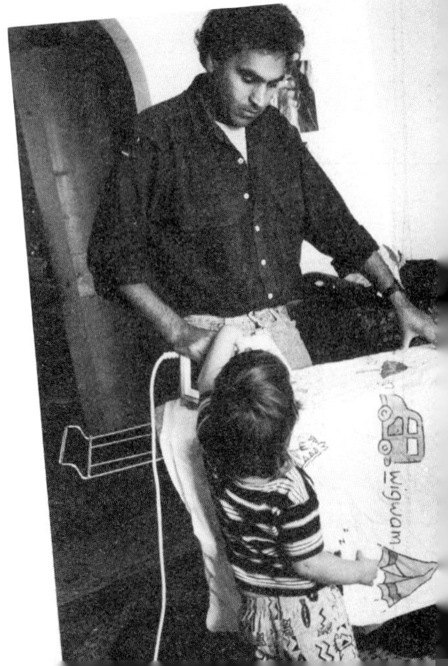

home. As I walked through the door my Dad was standing with his face to the wall, and Mum was sitting there crying her eyes out. It was the first time I had ever seen her cry, and I immediately stopped thinking of her as a great lady that no one or nothing could hurt.

As I went over to her I looked at her and talked to her in a voice that she always talked to me in when I was hurt. She managed a little smile but then broke down and cried again. She took hold of me and said, 'I'll never let it happen to you.'

I was puzzled but I didn't say anything for I knew questions would hurt her all the more.

When Dad turned round he looked ill and old. All my dreams of him being my hero in shining armour dropped as well. I never knew what had happened but it hurt me too, because now I knew I couldn't depend on them as much as I could before, when I knew they could be hurt too.

Carole Carr,
Age 13

...But sometimes the roles change. Who's helping who here?

Parents crying

1 How did the incident change the way Carol thought about her parents?

2 Did the incident change the way her parents thought about her?

3 Parents may not wish to share their problems with their children. Do children have a right to know?

Her parents' eyes

1 Why is Linda so important to her mother and father?

2 What sort of person do you think she is?

3 You plan to interview Linda for your school magazine. Make a list of 8 to 10 questions you would ask her about how she helps her parents every day.

4 Working with a partner, role play the interview, with one of you taking the part of Linda.

The Shed

There's a shed at the bottom of our garden
With a spider's web hanging across the door,
The hinges are rusty and creak in the wind.
When I'm in bed I lie and listen,
I'll open that door one day.

There's a dusty old window around at the side
With three cracked panes of glass,
I often think there's someone staring at me
Each time that I pass,
I'll peep through that window one day.

My brother says there's a ghost in the shed
Who hides under the rotten floorboards,
And if I ever dare to set foot inside
He'll jump out and chop off my head,
But I'll take a peek one day.

I know that there isn't really a ghost,
My brother tells lies to keep the shed for his den;
There isn't anyone staring or making strange noises
And the spider has been gone from his web since
I don't know when,
I'll go into that shed one day soon.

But not just yet...

Frank Flynn

Hidden away in a meadow, below the Wiltshire village of Bromham, is a rather special hide-away – an exceptional tree house.

The shed

1 How does the poet feel about the shed?

2 What do you think he finds in the shed when he eventually goes inside?

3 You and a group of friends have been given an old shed to use as a meeting place. Describe what the shed was like when you first took it over. Say how you repaired and repainted it, what you put in it and how you use it. Illustrate your description with drawings.

Tree house

Your family and a friend's family have decided to spend five days together, over Christmas, in a tree house.
The weather is awful: rain, fog, snow, and gales. As the weather gets worse, so do relationships between the two families.

1 Draw a diagram of the inside of the tree house. Mark where everyone sleeps, eats, cooks, watches TV, plays games, etc. Also draw in any special or unusual features of the tree house.

2 Write a diary of the five days spent in the tree house. Set it out like this:

Day 1

22 December
Whose idea was it to come here!!!!
Rained all day.
The roof leaks.
Mum in one of her moods.

Countdown

'Dial', said the poster,
6 5 4 3 2 1
For an unforgettable
Experience.

I lifted the receiver,
Put money
In the slot, dialled
The number;

The phone box
TOOK OFF!

Thundering flames
Shot me upwards,
Into the circle
Of a sapphire sky,

Above trees, houses,
Traffic, people,
Beyond birds,
Beyond clouds;

Into the clear
Blue stratosphere
Without a ticket –
I'm still up here,

Leaving Earth
At the speed of light,
Sending this message
By satellite.

Irene Rawnsley

Satellites

The planet Earth has one natural satellite, the Moon. There are also many artificial satellites in orbit round the Earth that have been put there by rockets. The word 'satellite' means 'something going in orbit round a larger object'. The natural satellites of the planets are often called moons, and the word satellite on its own usually means an artificial one.

A satellite's orbit is its path in space. The shape of the orbit is an ellipse. A satellite keeps going round a planet and does not fly off into space because the pull of gravity of the much bigger planet holds onto it.

What satellites are used for

Some Earth satellites are manned space stations where the crew can do scientific experiments and test the effects of weightlessness.

Unmanned satellites have many uses. Communications satellites relay telephone, television and radio signals between continents. Navigation satellites send out radio signals that help ships and aircraft work out their positions. Weather satellites photograph the cloud patterns for the forecasters. 'Spy' satellites take close-up photographs of the ground for military use.

Oxford Children's Encyclopedia

Madam

Madam
I have sold you
an electric plug
an electric torch
an electric blanket
an electric bell
an electric cooker
an electric kettle
an electric fan
an electric iron
an electric drier
an electric mixer
an electric washer
an electric peeler
an electric sweeper
an electric mower
an electric singer
an electric knife
an electric clock
an electric fire
an electric switch
an electric toothbrush
an electric razor
an electric teapot
an electric eye
an electric light.
Allow me to sell you
an electric chair.

Christopher Logue

Countdown

You are in the phone box, orbiting the Earth. The phone rings. You pick it up. Who is on the other end? What do they say to you? With your partner, role play the conversation you have with the mystery caller.

Satellites

1 The first artificial satellite was launched by Russia in 1957. In what ways have satellites changed our lives?

2 Can you think of any other ways satellites will be used in future?

Madam

1 How many appliances did 'madam' buy? Why did the assistant want to sell her an electric chair?

3 Make a list of all the appliances you or your group use in a week. Arrange them in order: most essential, useful, to least essential, luxury.

4 Design an advert for one of your essential appliances. What are its main benefits? Does it save time, money, effort, energy?

5 Design an advert for an appliance that might be on sale in the year 2500. This can be a futuristic version of an appliance used now. Or it might advertise a completely new product.

Robots at Home

We would all like to have a robot as a personal servant in the home. No more doing the dishes, making beds, tidying up your room, mowing the grass. We could leave it all to our home robot.

The idea of the domestic robot is very popular. People spend a lot of time doing boring home chores. If it is important to get robots to do the boring jobs in factories, is it not equally important to have them doing the dull tasks around the home, so that we can spend our time doing the things that we want to do instead?

Of course, not all people dislike housework that much. Some people even find that it is relaxing to do a simple cleaning task which does not need any thought after a day at work. But there must be few people who would not like to give some of their housework to a domestic servant.

In theory, it would be possible to make a useful home robot which could vacuum clean the carpet, cook a meal or mow the grass. Some people already claim to have done it.

But to train a robot to do such tasks at the moment would involve very much more work than doing the job yourself. And you would still have to keep a close eye on it to make sure that it did not do any damage by mistake.

Present-day robots are not nearly clever enough to deal with all the problems which they might come across in the course of doing a simple job. Would it notice the dog's bone lying in its way on the grass before it smashed the mower up by running over it?

What would it do if it could not find the cooking oil on the shelf? Would it know to look on the table and in the other cupboards? Would it know that it could use butter instead?

The Age of Computers, Robots and Intelligent Machines,
Ian Litterick

Domestic Help

The other day,
one of our domestic robots went mad,
kissed my dad,
poured marmalade over the videowall,
shampooed the cat,
sugared my mother's hair,
and sat on my sister's knee
(she fell through the chair).

Dad's frantic fiddling with the control-panel
only made matters worse.

It vacuum-cleaned the ceiling,
put the coffee-table into the garbage disposal unit,
uncorked a bottle of wine
and poured it gently over the carpet,
then carefully unscrewed its head
and deposited it in Mum's lap.

Mother says
that's the way it is these days:
you can't get the robots you used to.

Adrian Henri

Robots at home

1 Would you like to own a domestic robot?

2 What household jobs would you like it to do for you?

3 Why do you think present-day robots are 'not nearly clever enough'?

4 Design your own domestic robot. Label all its special features. Make a list of all the jobs it will do for you each day. Next to each job write down the number of hours it will take to do this job.

e.g. Cooking	4 hours
Washing up	2 hours

5 Use a calculator to help you to work out the total number of hours of extra free time you will have a year, if your robot does all these chores for you.

Domestic help

You volunteer to repair the domestic robot. You take it to pieces, put it back together again, but lose a vital part. When you switch it on you discover you've made it worse... and you cannot switch it off. Describe what the robot does to your bedroom.

Unlikely Inventions

Remarkable invention stories reach us frequently: this one comes from Russia. It's a pair of boots with a big difference. Each boot contains a small petrol engine. And the motors transmit so much power to the soles of the feet that whoever wears them can stride along in giant three-metre steps – that's at least three times bigger than normal. But Russian pedestrians aren't likely to rush off for a pair – the boots weigh almost six kilos, and you have to carry a can of petrol to keep them going. So they're not even as effective as seven-league boots in old fairy tales.

For those people who long to see themselves as others see them, an unusual product went on sale in America. It was called a Rorrim – that's mirror spelt backwards. Unlike ordinary mirrors, the rorrim shows a true reflection and doesn't reverse the image. So when you comb your hair, your parting on the left-hand side, appears on the right in the rorrim. And what's more, when you turn the rorrim upside down, it shows *you* upside down. Very confusing – especially for DNOURSWEN snaf!

And from Finland comes news of an invention to please animal lovers. It's a painless mousetrap, and it took its inventor *thirty years* to work out. The

trap looks like a box, and if a mouse touches the bait it will drop through a trapdoor, unharmed, into a cell below. The only trouble with this invention is that no one has suggested what you should *do* with the mouse once it was caught. Perhaps in another thirty years the inventor will provide the answer?

And Finally,
John Craven and Eric Rowan

Ladislao Biro

You may never have heard of Ladislao Biro, but you have certainly heard of the pen he invented – the ballpoint pen, or biro. Before Biro invented his pen, people wrote with fountain pens. The ink smudged and blotted and the pens sometimes leaked. In the 1930s Biro was a magazine editor in Budapest in Hungary. He noticed that the inks which the magazine's printers used dried very quickly. Biro wondered if quick-drying inks could be used in pens. He came up with the idea of a tube of ink with a free-moving ball on the end. As a person wrote, the ball collected ink from the tube and rolled it on to the paper. The pen would be cheap and could be thrown away when the ink ran out.

Biro began to work on his invention but before he could patent it the Second World War broke out. Biro left war-torn Europe and fled to Buenos Aires in Argentina. There, he and his brother Georg, who was a chemist, began to improve the pen. In the early 1940s Biro began to manufacture his new pen, the biro.

Biro did not have enough money to start a big manufacturing company. In 1944, he sold his invention to another company, who began to mass-produce the pen for the British and American armed forces. The servicemen and women liked the pens because they did not leak and were easy to carry around.

Biro was pleased that his pen was popular, but he did not gain much from his invention. The biro was later sold to the French firm, Bic, who now sell twelve million pens a day. Biro sank into obscurity in South America and it is not known whether he is still alive today. His name, however, has become a household word.

Twenty Inventors,
Jacqueline Dineen

Unlikely inventions

Think of some more 'unlikely' inventions. Pick one of them to describe in detail, with the help of some clearly labelled diagrams. The drawings should show the size of the invention, the materials it is made from and how it works.

Ladislao Biro

1 Did Ladislao Biro make a lot of money from his invention?

2 Why did people prefer his pen to fountain pens?

3 What is a 'patent'?

4 Pick one widely used everyday object, e.g. something like the ball-point pen, that you wish you had invented, and say why. Find out how it was invented.

Acknowledgements

The author and publisher are grateful to the following for permission to include copyright text, cartoons, and photos.

Cartoon Aid Ltd: Volley ball cartoon from *The Cartoon Aid Olympic Book* (1988). **Cassel PLC**: Jack to Jean', extract from *Naming Baby* by Eugene Stone (Ward Lock Ltd., 1981). **Collins & Brown Ltd.**: 'Bite Foils Tiger' from *Mrs Brown's Scrapbook* (1990). **Craven Images**: extracts from *And Finally* by John Craven and Eric Rowan (1984). **Alan Curless**: cartoon, 'Older Generations Manipulating the Young'. **Curtis Brown Ltd, New York**: X.J. Kennedy, 'Mixed-up School' and 'Unusual Shoelaces', © X.J. Kennedy. **Curtis Brown Ltd.**, on behalf of the author's estate: 'The Greater Cats', © Vita Sackville West. **Andre Deutsch Ltd.**: 'Here Are the Football Results' by Michael Rosen. **Faber & Faber Ltd.**: 'Biking', 'Cat' and 'Tiger' from *Midnight Forest* by Judith Nicholls, © Judith Nicholls 1987. **Frank Flynn**: 'The Shed', © Frank Flynn 1984, first published in *The Candy Floss Tree*: Poems by Norman Nicholson, Gerda Mayer and Frank Flynn (OUP, 1984). **Freemantle Arts Centre Press** (Australia and N.Z.)/**Virago Press**: extracts from *My Place* by Sally Morgan. **Victor Gollancz Ltd.**: Delia Elphon, 'How to Talk to Your Mother' from *Teenage Romance* (1986). **Paul Hamlyn Publishing** (part of **Reed International Books Ltd.**): extracts from *That's Life* (1989). **HarperCollins Publishers**: Peter Wesley Smith, 'Nomenclature' and 'God Made the Rivers' from *I'm Mad at You*; Anthony de Mello, 'Family Dinner' from *The Heart of Enlightenment*; 'We Doubt It' and 'It Looked That Way' from *Jokes, Quotes and One-liners for Public Speakers* by H.V. Prochnov and M.B. Prochnov Jr. (Thorsons, 1987, an imprint of HarperCollins Publishers Ltd.). **HarperCollins Publishers Inc.**: Shel Silverstein, 'Fancy Dive' from *A Light in the Attic*. **Headlands Press Inc.**, Tiburon, CA, USA: 'Hunker Hawser' from *New Games Book*, ed. Andrew Fleugelman. **Patricia Hubbell**: 'Shadows', © Patricia Hubbell, reprinted in *This Delicious Day*, ed. P.B. Janeczko (Orchard Books, 1987). **Lancaster Citizen**: 'Dogs to Get a Chip off the Old Doc!', *Lancaster Citizen*, 11.10.90. **Lennard Associates**: extracts from *Top Ten of Everything* by Russell Ash (1989). **Christopher Logue**: 'Madam', © Christopher Logue. **Methuen Children's Books**: 'Her Parent's Eyes' from *Front Page Kids* by Sarah Livinoff and Vida Adamoli (1987); 'Changing His Mind', 'Treasure Trove' and 'Mum, Dad and Me' from *Ask a Silly Question* by Irene Rawnsley. **Mulberry Editions**: 'Alphabet Tales' and 'Hidden Animals' from *Children's Travel Games* by Andrew Langley (1992). **National Extension College**: 'What Parents Say' from *The Parent Book* by Nancy Kohner. **Sheryl L. Nelms**: 'Real Talent', © Sheryl L. Nelms, from *This Delicious Day*, ed. P.B. Janeczko (Orchard Books, 1987). **The Open University**: cartoon,'Teenagers on the 'Phone', adapted from *Parents and Teenagers*, The Open University in association with the Health Education Council and Scottish Health Education Group (Harper, 1982). **Oxford University Press**: 'Satellites', 'Volleyball', 'Netball', 'Basketball', 'American Football', and 'Gymnastics' (illustrations by Jim Robbins) from *Oxford Children's Encyclopedia*, © OUP 1991; 'Keeping Fit' from *All About Health* by Dorothy Baldwin (1985). **Penguin Books Ltd.**: Kit Wright, 'Cleaning Ladies' and 'How I see It' from *Hot Dog*, © Kit Wright 1981, first published by Kestrel Books; Brian Patten, 'Snodding' from *Gargling With Jelly*, © Brian Patten 1985, first published by Viking Kestrel; Doug Macleod, 'Thank you, Dad, for Everything' from *The Fed-Up Family Album*, © Doug Macleod, 1983, first published by Kestrel Books, Australia; 'Ticklish Tomes' from *The End*, ed. Richard Stanley, © Richard Stanley, 1980, published in Puffin Books and by Kestrel Books, 1980. **Aidan Potts**: cartoon, 'Changing Heads'. **Punch**: cartoon, Ed McLachlan 'Action Words'. **Random House UK Ltd.**: 'Reasons for Having a Pet' from *How to Handle Grown-ups* by Jim and Duncan Eldridge (Beaver, 1985); 'School Jokes' and 'How to Get Out of Games' from *The Completely Misleading Guide to School* by Jim Eldridge (Red Fox, 1990). **Irene Rawnsley**: 'Countdown', © Irene Rawnsley. **Routledge**: extract from *Tales Out of School* by Roger White and David Brockington. **Caroline Sheldon Literary Agency**: cartoon, 'Mum the telly's gone funny again!' from *Rocking the Boat* by Helen Cusack, published by Futura Publications 1989. **Talmy Franklin Ltd.**: 'Enough Smiths' from *Would You Believe It?* by D. Sanders, Girling, Davies and R. Sanders (1974). **Today**: 'Why Sports Day Pupils Run a Mile' by David Lawson, *Today*, 25.6.91. **Watson Little Ltd., Authors' Agents**: 'The Rebel' by D.J. Enright, first published in *Rhyme Times Rhyme* (Chatto and Windus). **Wayland (Publishers) Ltd.**: from *Twenty Inventors* by Jacqueline Dineen (1988). **The Women's Press Ltd.**: Anna Swir, 'I'm Panting' from *Fat Like the Sun* (1986).

Every effort has been made to secure all permissions prior to publication. If contacted, the publisher will be pleased to rectify any errors or omissions at the earliest opportunity.

The illustrations are by Martin Chatterton pp. 14, 15, 40, 61, 62; Elitta Fell p. 33; Sophie Grillet pp. 4/5, 11, 36/7, 60; Ann Johns pp. 24, 25; Antony Lee pp. 16 (bottom), 18, 27, 59; Diane Lumley pp. 30, 50; Joanna Martin pp. 52, 53; John Morris p. 12; Martin Sanders p. 41; Dee Shulman pp. 16 (top); 20; Adam Stower pp. 6/7, 48/9, 56/7.

The publishers would like to thank the following for permission to reproduce photographs:
Shaun Botterill/Allsport UK Ltd. p. 47, Dan Smith/Allsport UK Ltd. p. 42; Jean-Paul Ferrero/Ardea London Ltd. p. 9 (bottom left); Judy Harrison/Format p. 54; Harry Philpott p. 55; Simon Thompson/Photofusion p. 29 (bottom); Popperfoto p. 63; Nasa/Science Photo Library p. 58; Sporting Pictures p. 44; Topham pp. 4, 9 (top and middle left), 29 (top left), 33, 39, 57; John Walmsley p. 36.